Learning Tree 1 2 3

What's the Difference?

By Richard and Nicky Hales
Illustrated by Rebecca Archer

Geddes+ Grosset

As you read this book, try to answer the questions, and try to think of some questions of your own.
Write your answers on a piece of paper or in a notebook – not in the book.
There are answers at the end of the book. Try not to look at them before you have had a try. If you find the questions difficult, ask a grown-up or an older friend to help you.

First published in hardback 1991
Copyright © Cherrytree Press Ltd 1991

This paperback edition first published 1991 by
Geddes & Grosset Ltd
David Dale House
New Lanark ML11 9DJ

ISBN 1 85534 463 7

Printed and bound in Italy by L.E.G.O. s.p.a., Vicenza

All rights reserved. No part of this publication may be reproduced, stored in a retrieval system, or transmitted, in any form or by any means without the prior permission in writing of the publisher, nor otherwise circulated in any form of binding or cover other than that in which it is published and without a similar condition including this condition being imposed on the subsequent purchaser.

We are twins.
We both like swimming.
We are almost the same.

Can you see a difference between us?

Look at these two pictures.
Are they the same?

Can you find six differences between them?

Odd one out

Which is the odd one out?

Why is it different?

Which of these is odd? Why?

Which of these is odd? Why?

What's odd?

Find four different objects.
Any will do.

Now choose one object from the four.
Look at it carefully.
Think why it could be the odd one out.
Think why the other things might be odd.

How many?

How many frogs are there?
How many rubber rings are there?

Does every frog have a ring?

How many frogs are there?
How many beach-balls are there?

How many frogs haven't got a ball?

Matching

Cut out some paper frogs.
Cut up some straws.
Line up your frogs.
Match them with straws.

How many do not match up?
This is how you find the difference.

Find the difference between these.

More or less?

How many frogs are diving?
How many frogs are swimming?

How many more frogs are swimming than diving?

How many frogs are sliding?
How many frogs are floating?

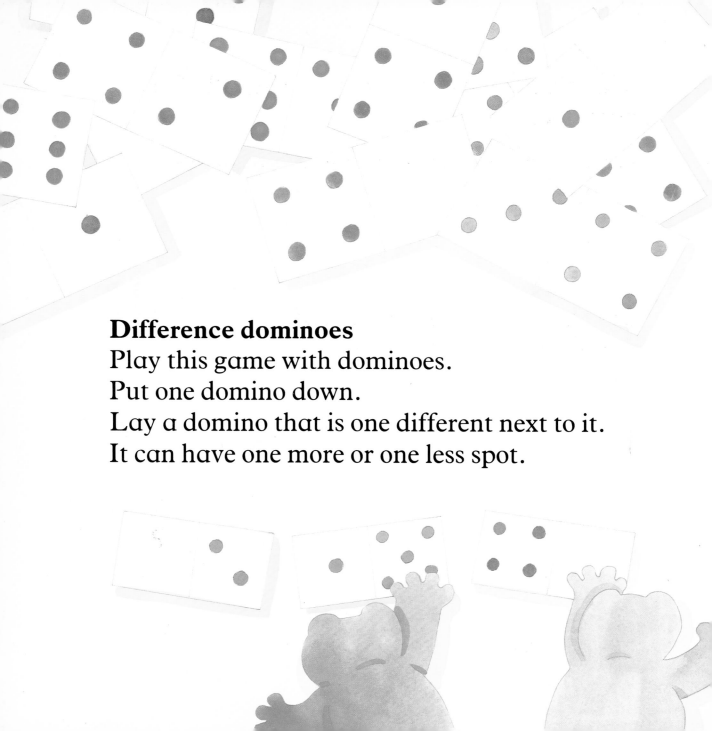

Difference dominoes

Play this game with dominoes.
Put one domino down.
Lay a domino that is one different next to it.
It can have one more or one less spot.

The winner is the first person to lay all of his dominoes.

Now try playing two-difference dominoes.

Try making a circle of one-difference dominoes.

Patterns of difference

Find the difference between:

1 and 2	2 and 3
1 and 3	2 and 4
1 and 4	2 and 5
1 and 5	2 and 6
1 and 6	2 and 7

Write your answers on a piece of paper.
Can you see a pattern in the answers?

Find the difference between:

2 and 4   1 and 3
2 and 6   1 and 5
2 and 8   1 and 7
2 and 10   1 and 9
2 and 12   1 and 11

What do you notice?

Now try this. What do you notice?

10 and 9
10 and 8
10 and 7
10 and 6
10 and 5
10 and 4
10 and 3
10 and 2
10 and 1
10 and 0

Snap the difference

You need a pack of cards.
Take out all the picture cards.

Deal the other cards out face up two at a time.

The first player to call out the difference between the two numbers takes both cards. The winner is the player who ends up with the most cards.

More things to do

Look out

Look out for differences. Does your house have more doors than windows? Do you have more sheets than pillows? Do you have more socks than shoes? Do you have more chips than sausages? Do you have more sisters than brothers? What is the difference in your ages?

Dominoes

If you haven't got any dominoes, you can make a set. Cut oblongs from stiff card. Make them twice as long as they are wide. Divide them in half and draw on the spots.

There are 28 dominoes in all. One domino has no spots. Six dominoes have no spots on one end. The other 21 have between one and six spots. Can you work out the patterns? If you can't, there is a picture of them on page 23.

Once you have made your dominoes, try playing three-difference dominoes. Can you make a three-difference circle?

Dice

Throw two dice and call out the difference between the two numbers. If you haven't got any dice you can make some like this.

Cut a circle of card (about 7 cm wide) and divide it into six sections. Mark each section with spots or a number from one to six. Then cut straight across the round edges. Push a cocktail stick through the middle and your dice is ready to spin. Read off the number where it comes to rest. Use two spinners together to play 'spot the difference'.

Tiddlywinks

Use a saucer instead of a pot for this game. Line up six tiddlywinks in a row. Try to flip them one by one into the saucer. See how many more land in the saucer than outside it. Keep trying until you can get them all in the saucer with one flip each.

1

1 Do you have more toes or more arms?

2 Which has more wheels: a bicycle or a car?

3 How many wheels has a tricycle? How many more wheels does a car have?

4 What is the difference between the spots on the green frog's domino? What is the difference between the spots on the blue frog's?

2

5 Four frogs have come to tea. There is one bun and two biscuits. Will every frog get something to eat?

6 What is the difference between the spots on these dominoes?

7 Which has more legs: a monkey or an ant?

8 Which is the odd one out: gloves, shoes, socks, hat?

9 What number comes next in this series: two, four, six? What is the difference between the numbers?

10 Can you sort a set of dominoes into groups according to the difference between the spots? Here is a group with a difference of four.

11 How many groups of dominoes are there? How many dominoes are there in each group?

12 Which of these numbers is the odd one out: two, four, five, six, eight? Why?

13 Find the difference between these pairs of numbers:

3 and 7	6 and 1
2 and 9	8 and 3
5 and 10	4 and 0

14 Find the difference between these:

10 and 8	3 and 10
4 and 10	10 and 2
10 and 1	0 and 10

15 Find the difference between these numbers. Use a calculator to help you.

21 and 12	65 and 56
32 and 23	76 and 67
43 and 34	

What do you notice about the answers?

Answers to 1 2 3

1 8 more toes
2 car
3 3
4 1
1
2
5 no (not unless they share)
6 4
4
7 ant
8 hat
9 8
2
10 –

11 7 groups of differences:

12 5 (cannot be divided by two)
13 4
5
5
4
7
14 2
6
8
9
10
15 all the answers are 9

Index

Answers

Page 3
One has to wear arm bands.

Page 4 & 5
Six differences:
One blue frog has changed its costume; one rail is missing from the steps; one yellow frog is missing; the ball has changed colour; one orange frog has changed its costume; the towel has changed colour.

Page 6
The ball is odd in a set of animals.
The frog is odd in a set of objects.

Page 7
The ice-cream is odd in a set of fruit.
The pepper-pot is odd in a set of cutlery.
The plate is odd in a set of drinking vessels.
The bucket is odd in a set of clothes.

Pages 8 & 9
Only the egg has a shell. You can eat the skin of an apple but not of the others.

Page 10
4 frogs
3 rings
No

Page 11
5 frogs
3 balls
2 frogs

Page 12
2 don't match up

Page 13
top: 3 don't match up
below: 2,5,3,3,5

Page 14
4 swimming
2 diving
2 more frogs swimming than diving

Page 15
5 sliding
2 floating
3 more sliding than floating

Page 18
1	1
2	2
3	3
4	4
5	5

Page 19
2	2
4	4
6	6
8	8
10	10

1, 2, 3, 4, 5, 6, 7, 8, 9, 10